THE TURNER COLLECTION IN THE CLORE GALLERY

The Turner Collection in the Clore Gallery

AN ILLUSTRATED GUIDE

Published to celebrate
the opening of the Gallery by
Her Majesty The Queen
1 April 1987

THE TATE GALLERY

cover
The Dogano, San Giorgio, Citella,
from the steps of the Europa
1842 (detail)

frontispiece
Self-portrait c.1799

The works on pages 23, 49 (bottom), 87,
91 (top) and 97 are reproduced by courtesy
of the Trustees of the National Gallery.

ISBN 0 946590 68 0 (paper)
ISBN 0 946590 69 9 (cloth)
Published by order of the Trustees 1987
Copyright © 1987 The Tate Gallery All rights reserved
Designed and published by Tate Gallery Publications,
Millbank, London SW1P 4RG
Printed in Great Britain by Balding + Mansell UK Limited

Contents

The Turner Collection in The Clore Gallery

Joseph Mallord William Turner was born in 1775, and died in 1851. His lifespan embraced what was perhaps the most fruitful of all periods in British art – an age that began with the achievements of Hogarth, Reynolds, Gainsborough and Wilson, continued into the epoch of high Romanticism, of Blake, Lawrence, Constable and Bonington, and concluded amid the novelties of Pre-Raphaelitism and Victorian realism. Turner himself seems in retrospect to preside over the whole period as the greatest figure of a host of great men, the culmination, almost the definition of the Romantic artist. He grew up when the Royal Academy was newly founded and the British school still rather self-consciously unsure of its credentials; his death coincided almost exactly with the date prophesied by John Constable when in 1822 he wrote: 'The art will go out: there will be no genuine painting in England in thirty years.'

Turner's Gallery

Turner was a professional artist from his earliest youth. He first began to exhibit his work publicly when he was still a boy, hanging watercolours in the window of his father's barber-shop in Maiden Lane, Covent Garden, and selling them for a few shillings each. At the age of fifteen, in 1790, he sent one of his views to the Royal Academy, where it was shown in the summer exhibition that year. Thereafter, for the rest of his life, he regularly submitted paintings and watercolours to the Academy. But the desire to keep his work before the public was not satisfied by this. In 1799, the year in which he was elected an Associate of the Academy, he took rooms in a house in Harley Street where, by 1804, he had built himself a gallery in which he could display twenty or thirty pictures. Here, for a number of years, he held his own annual exhibitions. In 1810 he moved to a house close by, at 47 Queen Anne Street West: to this, too, he added a gallery, which was finished in 1821 to his own careful designs and hung with dark red paper. But whereas in his early days he had announced regular exhibitions and, while he prohibited sketching, encouraged the public to view, in his later life he was reclusive and jealous of his privacy. It became a matter of fascination among art-lovers to contrive access to Turner's Gallery, and there is a fund of anecdote and reminiscence describing the eccentric conditions in which the artist lived:

> The door was opened by a woman, for whom one hardly knew what to feel most, terror or pity . . . She showed us into a dining-room, which had penury and meanness written on every wall and article of furniture. Then up into the gallery; a fine room – indeed, one of the best in London, but in a dilapidated state; his pictures the same. The great 'Rise of Carthage' all mildewed and flaking off; . . . he uncovered a few matchless creatures, fresh and dewy, like pearls just set – the mere colours grateful to the eye without reference to the subjects . . . The old gentleman was great fun . . .

After the death of his father in 1829 Turner made his first will. He was fifty-four years old and at the height of his career, but the personal tragedy made him newly conscious of the uncertainty of life and the need to make explicit his complicated plans. He bequeathed two of the most celebrated of his earlier masterpieces to the National Gallery, on condition that they should always hang between two paintings by his great French predecessor Claude Lorraine. The pictures in question, 'Dido building Carthage' and 'The decline of Carthage', were both works that owed much to the seventeenth-century master. They announced, in fact, that Turner's lifelong ambition to emulate and surpass Claude had, in his own estimation, been realised. It was a gesture of triumph.

He never changed the terms of this unusual bequest to the National Gallery, although he had at one point, perhaps jokingly, expressed the wish to be buried in the canvas of 'Dido building Carthage'. But in a new will of 1831 he changed the second of the two pictures to 'Sun rising through vapour'. He soon had further thoughts about the rest of his large output. His fellow Academician the architect Sir John Soane was in the process of having a Bill passed by Parliament to permit him to leave his house in Lincoln's Inn Fields to the public as a museum. The idea obviously attracted Turner, who in August 1832 drafted a strange, muddled codicil to his will in which he directed that funds were to be made available from his estate 'for the erection of the Gallery to hold my Pictures' and for the accommodation of one or more custodians. This was to be done 'keeping in view the first objects I direct namely is to keep my pictures together so that they may be seen known or found at the discretion'. He continued: 'as to the mode how they may be viewed gratuitously I leave to my Executors'. The wording is unclear but it seems that Turner intended this new gallery to form part of a 'Charitable Institution for the Maintenance and Support of Male Decayed Artists' for which he had provided in his original will. If this Charity were not instituted, he directed his Executors 'to keep all the Pictures and Property in Queen Ann St West No 47 intire and unsold' and to maintain them there as 'Turner's Gallery'. He appointed his long-standing housekeeper Hannah Danby as 'Custodian and Keeper of the Pictures Houses and Premises', while the Executors were 'to keep the said Gallery in a viewable state at all times concurring with the object of keeping my works together and to be seen under certain restrictions which may be most reputable and advisable'. This odd document was never attested, and is, at best, only a vague foreshadowing of ideas that were to crystallise in his mind much later. They received an important catalyst in 1847, when the collector Robert Vernon gave a large group of modern British pictures to the National Gallery, among them four by Turner. Although lack of space prevented the Trustees displaying Vernon's collection, they did hang one work – Turner's Venetian view of 'The Dogano, San Giorgio, Citella, from the steps of the Europa'. These developments seem to have provided the clarification needed for his own intentions, and on 2 August 1848 he added a new, and properly drafted, codicil to his will. This specified that the works with which he was concerned were his 'finished pictures' – about 100 of these were counted in his studio after his death. It was this group that he insisted must be 'kept together'. 'Sun rising through vapour' and 'Dido building Carthage' were to go to the National Gallery as originally planned; but now all the finished pictures were also 'bequeathed unto the Trustees of the National Gallery provided that a room or rooms are added to the present National Gallery to be when erected called "Turner's Gallery" in which such pictures are to be constantly kept deposited and preserved'. If these conditions were not met the pictures were to remain at Queen Anne Street, under the guardianship of Hannah Danby (or a successor to be appointed by the Trustees) until the lease of the property could no longer be renewed; then they were to be sold. Turner made no mention of the remaining contents of his studio and gallery – some 180 oil sketches and over 19,000 drawings, many in sketch books, so it may be assumed that these were intended to be sold as part of the estate. As an afterthought he added to this codicil the proviso that, following the expiry of the Queen Anne Street lease, the National Gallery might have five years to construct the new 'Turner Gallery', or forfeit the pictures. A further codicil of 1 February 1849 modified this slightly, declaring the gift void if the Trustees of the National Gallery had not provided accommodation for the pictures ten years after Turner's death. The proceeds from the sale of the pictures were to be divided between the Royal Academy Pension Fund, the Artist's General Benevolent Fund and, of course, his own Institution for Decayed Artists.

He died on 19 December 1851 at the age of 76. He was buried according to his wishes in St Paul's Cathedral 'among my Brothers in Art' and the will and codicils were proved on 6 September 1852. His effects were valued at £140,000. By living frugally and carefully husbanding the profits of his successful practice as a painter and illustrator he had amassed a large fortune, partly, no doubt, for the charitable objects explained in his will and codicils. His family, however, had received nothing: a few small bequests and annuities to uncles and cousins, and to his illegitimate daughters Evelina and Georgiana, were revoked in the 1848 codicil. His relatives now sued Turner's executors for what they judged their fair share of his money, arguing, among other things, that he was not of sound mind when he made his dispositions, and seizing on a technical flaw in the wording of the original will. The case dragged on until 1856 when, in a compromise settlement given effect by a Decree of the Court of Chancery dated 19 March, all the pictures, drawings and sketches in the artist's hand found in his possession at the time of his death were made over to 'the Trustees for the Time being of the National Gallery', to be retained by them 'for the Benefit of the Public'. Such money as was left in the estate after the payment of legal costs and the carrying out of various minor directives in the will (such as the erection of a monument in St Paul's) went to Turner's relations.

The Turner Bequest

Although the Trustees of the National Gallery did what they could to exhibit a representative selection of Turner's Bequest, designating part of their building in Trafalgar Square 'Turner's Gallery', and showing them with watercolours chosen and annotated by Ruskin at the new South Kensington Museum, no separate accommodation for the collection was provided until the opening of an annexe for the national collection of British Art at Millbank, the Tate Gallery, in 1897. Here, in 1910, Sir Joseph Duveen generously built the suite of galleries which until now have housed Turner's pictures, and which may be said to have belatedly fulfilled almost all the conditions Turner laid down in his will. The finished oil paintings, and indeed the unfinished ones, together with many sketches in oil and watercolour, have been exhibited in changing displays, as he envisaged.

Meanwhile the watercolours and selected pages from the sketchbooks were shown in various museums and galleries in the 'loan collections' originally assembled by Ruskin in the 1850s and 1860s. Despite Ruskin's warnings these had, over the years, unfortunately been subjected to considerable exposure to uncontrolled daylight with the result that a number of sheets were damaged by fading or discolouration. The Tate Gallery housed all the works on paper in its basement, and a disastrous flooding of the Thames in January 1928 completely submerged them. A few items were lost, and much incidental damage incurred, but thanks to the prompt action of a few dedicated helpers the great majority of drawings were saved. As a consequence of the accident, however, they were removed to higher ground and by 1931 had joined the national collection of works on paper in the Department of Prints and Drawings at the British Museum. They have continued to be shown in frequent travelling exhibitions and in various displays in London, though in recent decades scrupulous care has been taken to minimise the dangers of exposure to excessive light.

In 1974–5 a large exhibition held at the Royal Academy to celebrate the bicentenary of Turner's birth brought together many oils, watercolours and sketchbooks from the Bequest, with prints and pictures lent from collections throughout the world. The exhibition prompted a new urge to see the range of his output under one roof, and – although he had never explicitly given so many of his works to the Nation – it was felt that the only way in which full justice could be done to his many-sided genius was for a new gallery to be found in which provision was made for the display of all aspects of his art. In 1980 a magnificent offer by the Clore Foundation made it possible for the Trustees of the Tate Gallery to commission a new wing of the building for that purpose.

The Clore Gallery from the Tate Gallery Steps

Room 107 looking
towards Rooms 104 and 101

The Main Entrance from
the Garden Terrace

The Clore Gallery

The Clore Gallery, designed by James Stirling, Michael Wilford and Associates, shows Turner's work in a suite of eight principal rooms, with an adjoining gallery for watercolours from which daylight is excluded. Three further rooms on the floor above provide space for the hanging of the remainder of the oil paintings as a reserve collection, so that in practice all the works in oil are easily accessible. The Trustees of the National Gallery have generously agreed to allow seven works normally exhibited at Trafalgar Square to join the remainder of the collection for several months. Among them are some of the most famous of Turner's canvases, including 'Calais Pier', 'The Fighting Temeraire' and 'Rain, Steam and Speed', which contribute important focal points for the periods in which they were painted. As Turner wished, the display of pictures in the principal rooms will occasionally be changed; and there will be a regular series of temporary exhibitions of the watercolours and other works on paper in the watercolour room. Works on paper not actually on show, including a representative collection of prints after Turner's designs, can be examined in the Study Room on the second floor. Visitors have access to a photographic index of the entire collection, a microfilm reader and a library of reference material. The Tate Gallery's collection of British drawings and watercolours up to 1900 may also be studied here. In this way the Clore Gallery provides a comprehensive survey of the whole of Turner's output in its context, from his earliest surviving sketches to his latest exhibited masterpieces; the complete range of his sketchbooks (only four are known to be in collections elsewhere) and thousands of colour studies, in both oil and watercolour, give an exceptionally complete insight into his creative processes. A display of personal relics and documents, in room 103, adds a further, biographical dimension to the presentation of the man as well as the artist.

Model Ships
As one of Turner's friends recalled, in the artist's home 'There
were several models of ships in glass cases, to which Turner had
painted a sea and background. They much resembled the vessels
in his sea pieces.'

Studio Cabinet,
A large mahogany portable
cabinet containing sixteen
jars of dry pigments, principally reds,
yellows and browns.

Metal paint box
A box containing glass tubes
of dry pigments and small bags
of pigment pastes in drying
oil and resin.

A travelling
watercolour case.
Apparently improvised
by Turner himself from the
cover of an almanac.

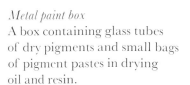

A small box holding four glass
bottles of paint thinners and vehicles;
one is labelled 'Acetate of morphia', which
does not appear to have been used in painting.

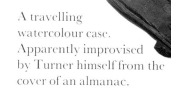

High Art and the Sublime

Turner had been practising as a watercolourist for nearly a decade when he sent his first oil painting to the Royal Academy's spring exhibition in 1796. In both medium and subject-matter 'Fishermen at sea' marked a new departure: the heaving surface of the sea and effect of moonlight were themes that he had experimented with in earlier drawings but never rendered with such consummate polish. It is a canvas that throws down the gauntlet to the most accomplished landscape and marine painters of the day, and proclaims its superiority to them all. The exhibited pictures of the next few years, before and after his election first as Associate (1799) and then as full member (1802) of the Academy, continued to be ambitious in conception and, increasingly, in scale as well. The first of the principal galleries presents his work of this period, and shows him deliberately aiming to overawe his audience according to the demands of the 'Grand Style'. The eighteenth-century theory of the Sublime held that serious art should deal with the noblest and most powerful themes and Turner set out to show that landscape could meet these high expectations. He began with landscape subjects of a picturesquely dramatic order, drawing on his travels in the north of England: 'Buttermere lake, with part of Cromackwater, Cumberland, a shower' is one of the finest of these, with its assured evocation of the scale of the Lakeland hills and their grand, if fleeting, climatic effects. But many of the most significant stages of his development at this period were marked by ambitious marines. 'Calais Pier', shown in 1803, was painted just after he had been elected Royal Academician, and reflects the influence of the sea-pieces of Ruysdael that he had seen during his visit to Paris in 1802. It nevertheless records a personal experience, Turner's landing at Calais – and is the first of a long and important sequence of pictures, produced at different times in the artist's life, which are inspired by the incidents of his tireless travelling. A still more vividly immediate rendering of the violence of the sea followed in the celebrated 'Shipwreck' which Turner showed in 1805, where his concern with the plight of human beings at the mercy of nature is revealed in carefully individualised figures and lively characterisation.

In a more generalised and still grander idiom, he went on to produce scenes illustrating cataclysms from Biblical or ancient history. Three of these dominate the room: 'The destruction of Sodom', possibly shown at

Fishermen at Sea
1796 (detail)

Turner's own gallery in 1805, but apparently left unfinished; 'The Deluge' of about the same date, and 'Snow storm: Hannibal and his army crossing the Alps' which appeared at the Academy in 1812. Less turbulent though equally disturbing in its way is 'Apollo and Python', shown in 1811, which displays in allegorical guise the struggle of light and darkness, good and evil.

To many of these pictures Turner appended appropriate quotations from Milton, Thomson and other literary sources, amplifying the ideas propounded in the compositions themselves. In the case of 'Hannibal', the verses he published were of his own making, and were attributed to a 'Manuscript Poem, Fallacies of Hope'. The 'Fallacies of Hope' was to alternate with Thomson and Byron in Turner's catalogue entries for the remainder of his life, but it seems never to have reached a final or definitive form; indeed, it is rather a collective title for a group of fragments written to explicate the pictures than a coherent work in its own right. The artist's notebooks of the first decade of the century are full of jottings towards poems which rarely achieved completion and, despite the evident seriousness with which Turner regarded these essays, it has to be admitted that they betray no great literary talent.

The allusions to more enduring works of literature are wide-ranging. Milton was the modern British equivalent of Homer and Virgil, and Turner evoked his *Paradise Lost* as well as the Bible when he painted the dark, swirling 'Deluge' with its heroic, large-scale figures. An even more recent poet who engrossed his interest later was Byron: the first time Byron's work was quoted by Turner was in connection with his highly-charged nocturne 'The Field of Waterloo', shown at the Academy in 1818. This intensely romantic meditation on the suffering and loss occasioned by war is perhaps Turner's most forceful comment on a man-made rather than a natural catastrophe, and brings to an end the sequence of large early canvases in which he continues the tradition of painting historical subjects in dark tones on a dark ground.

Calais Pier, with French poissards preparing for sea : an
English packet arriving

1803 $67\frac{3}{4} \times 94\frac{1}{2}$ (172 × 240)

Turner scribbled on a sketch for this picture 'Our landing at
Calais. Nearly swampt'. His sea storms always derive from
vividly felt personal experience, and his carefully worded titles
(compare the 'Snowstorm: steam-boat off a harbour's mouth' of
1842) further emphasise the precise realism at which he aims.
But while it attempts complete conviction 'Calais Pier' is also a
work in the grand manner, and Turner has one eye fixed firmly
on the Dutch seventeenth-century sea painters, Backhuysen and
Ruysdael.

Shipwreck

1805 $67\frac{1}{8} \times 95\frac{1}{8}$ (170.5 × 241.5)

After 'Fishermen at Sea' of 1796 Turner regularly produced
marine subjects, which became steadily grander and stormier
over the next decade or so. In 1805 he showed this, one of the
finest of them, which was so much admired that it was shortly
afterwards engraved with great success, his first painting to be
reproduced in this way. The graphic realism of swirling water,
lurching vessels and terrified people announces Turner's
intention not merely of entertaining his audience but of
convincing us that what he tells us is the truth of nature and
man's relationship to it.

Snow Storm: Hannibal and his army crossing the Alps

1812   36 × 48 (91.5 × 122)

This, the culminating work in the sequence of natural
cataclysms that Turner painted in the first half of his career,
appeared at the Academy in 1812. It is said to have been
inspired by a thunderstorm that Turner had witnessed in
Yorkshire a year or two earlier; but if it relies on personal
experience it transcends any local or chronological boundaries in
the overwhelming vision of titanic struggle that it presents: man
contends with man, and armies battle with the elements; human
ambition is checked by the forces of nature. Turner may well
have had a modern example in mind: Hannibal's invasion of
Italy is perhaps a metaphor for the overweening career of
Napoleon.

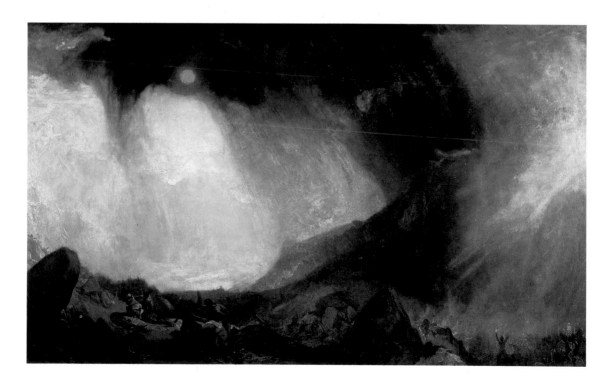

Apollo and Python

1811 $57\frac{1}{4} \times 93\frac{1}{2}$ (145.5 × 237.5)

If Turner chose historical and mythological subjects to conform
to Academic expectations of serious art, he inevitably gave them
distinctly personal meanings. In this dramatic canvas, evidently
inspired by the ruggedly romantic landscapes of Salvator Rosa,
he retells the story of the sun god Apollo's defeat of the dragon
Python in terms of the bold opposition of light to darkness, good
to evil.

The field of Waterloo

1818   58 × 94 (147.5 × 239)

Turner visited Belgium in 1817, and showed this canvas at the
Academy the following year. It is the reverse of a conventional
battle picture, deliberately using the expected broad sweep of
countryside and clutter of bodies to make a poignant and quite
unheroic point: by the light of search flares, women wander the
battlefield looking for their menfolk among the dead of both
sides. The farm buildings of Hougoumont still burn in the
darkness, and colourful uniforms glitter with ironic brightness.
The horror of war is presented as an individual and personal
tragedy in a composition of great power and theatricality.

The Deluge

1805 $56\frac{1}{4} \times 92\frac{3}{4}$ (143 × 235)

Noah's flood was a popular subject among neo-classical and
romantic artists; the classic statement of the theme was
Poussin's, which Turner admired (and criticised) in the Louvre
in 1802. His own version, perhaps shown at his own gallery in
1805, seems to allude to the seventeenth-century master in its
deliberately bold and conspicuous groups of tangled figures.
The landscape itself is caught up in an apocalyptic storm of the
greatest violence, through which the stable triangle of the ark is
glimpsed as an unattainable haven in the midst of universal
destruction.

The Fall of an Avalanche in the Grisons

1810 $32\frac{1}{2} \times 47\frac{1}{4}$ (90 × 120)

A picture first shown at Turner's own gallery in 1810; he
composed several lines of blank verse to assist its impact and
underline the tragic implications of the event, which is not
simply a grand natural spectacle but a human catastrophe:

> ... extinction follows,
> And the toil, the hope of man – o'erwhelms.

Turner may have been thinking of an avalanche which had
killed twenty-five people in a cottage at Selva in Switzerland in
1808.

England and Working Life

The ideas for many of these subjects emerged as much from the artist's experience of nature as from his reading or study of the old masters. In about 1805 he took a house on the Thames outside London, at Isleworth, where he could meditate on the heroic past in a gentle English setting of trees and water. A sketchbook he used at the time, *Studies for Pictures; Isleworth* contains visions of Classical seaports alternating with records of stretches of the Thames, and graphically illustrates his parallel interests and the way fresh observation fertilised his grand themes. The following year he moved to Hammersmith, and in 1807 bought a plot of land at Twickenham a little further upstream. The landscape of the Thames naturally became an important source of inspiration in these years, and he produced a series of oil studies, some apparently executed, according to the new fashion among landscape painters, out of doors and direct on to canvas or wooden panel (see Room 103). Many of the finished works reflect these new interests: 'Ploughing up turnips, near Slough', of 1809, illustrates his ability to combine a sensitive account of the realities of rural life with the subtlest evocation of misty light. It is an entirely original work which nevertheless pays homage to the atmospheric effects of a seventeenth-century Dutch artist like Aelbert Cuyp.

A similarly personal reinterpretation of the Dutch tradition appears in 'Dorchester Mead, Oxfordshire', of 1810, and, altogether differently, in the large marine of 'Spithead: boat's crew recovering an Anchor' of 1808, which records the recent arrival of two Danish ships captured at the battle of Copenhagen. It restates Turner's interest in the art of van de Velde and van de Cappelle in terms that foreshadow the long sequence of subjects from the Dutch wars that he was to produce in the second half of his career.

The influence of seventeenth-century Holland appears in another guise at this time: Turner's attention had been directed to the interior genre subjects of Ostade and Teniers by the work of the young Scottish painter David Wilkie who in 1806 showed at the Academy a scene of 'Village Politicians', to great acclaim. Turner's innate competitiveness was stirred to emulation and in 1807 he sent to the exhibition his own rustic genre piece, 'A country blacksmith disputing upon the price of iron, and the price charged to the butcher for shoeing his poney' – a title that seems to reprove Wilkie for the imprecision of his own, and illustrates Turner's lifelong

A country blacksmith disputing upon the price of iron, and the price charged to the butcher for shoeing his pony
1807 (detail)

insistence on the documentary truth of his art, particularly as it relates to the trades and pastimes of ordinary people. The same vivid realism pervades numerous lesser works of these years: rural life takes precedence over the landscape in which it is carried on; and Turner's watercolours frequently show fairgrounds and markets swarming with life and activity. There is a similar immediacy in two very different works: the celebrated 'Frosty Morning' exhibited in 1813 and the large sea-piece of 1819, 'Entrance of the Meuse: Orange-merchant on the Bar, going to pieces; Brill Church bearing S.E. by S. Masensluys E. by S.' This last canvas, which is prophetic of developments in romantic marine painting over the ensuing twenty years, takes the tradition of the great Dutch sea-painters to an ambiguous climax of grandeur and comedy with its broad cloudscape, clownish sailors and bobbing oranges; its title once again reveals Turner's abiding anxiety to convince us that what he paints is the literal truth.

Another grand canvas of these years is the even larger 'England: Richmond Hill, on the Prince Regent's Birthday', exhibited in 1819. A glorious summer view from one of Turner's favourite vantage-points, the top of Richmond Hill, this work brings together many of his principal interests: the bourgeois entertainments of a summer day just outside London are presented as a *fête champêtre à la* Watteau, in a landscape of Claudian expansiveness and grace.

*Entrance of the Meuse : Orange-merchant on the Bar, going to
pieces ; Brill Church bearing S.E. by S., Masensluys E. by S.*

1819   69 × 97 (175.5 × 246.5)

Turner had visited Holland in 1817, and in 1818 painted his
famous view of 'Dort or Dordrecht' (Yale Center for British Art)
in the spirit of Cuyp. Although he still has the Dutch marine
artists in mind, Turner here strips his subject of the grandiose
connotations of the old masters. The fresh open-air mood of his
English subjects of the 1810s, and especially of his smaller,
informal marines, is presented on a grander scale in this large
canvas of 1819. Although it treats of a wreck it is not an exercise
in the Sublime, rather a study of clouds over the sea, with a
minor and somewhat comic incident taking place on the choppy
water.

Frosty morning

1813 $44\frac{3}{4} \times 68\frac{3}{4}$ (113.5 × 174.5)

There is a strong element of the autobiographical in this picture: the scene is one that Turner saw from a coach while travelling in Yorkshire, and the coach is visible in the far distance on the straight road to the left. The little girl who huddles for warmth in her rabbit-skin stole is supposed to be his elder daughter Evelina, while the patient horse in the traces of the labourer's cart is a portrait of Turner's own 'Crop-ear'. The rendering of the thick rime on earth and plants in the foreground is a *tour de force*, while the starkness of the composition seems to express the numbness of perception on a freezing winter morning.

A country blacksmith disputing upon the price of iron, and the price charged to the butcher for shoeing his pony

1807 $21\frac{5}{8} \times 30\frac{5}{8}$ (55 × 78)

In 1806 the young Scottish painter David Wilkie exhibited for the first time at the Academy: his picture, *Village Politicians*, was a resounding success and gave new currency to the seventeenth-century Dutch 'low-life' genre subjects which had been eclipsed for many decades by the demand for heroic art. Turner seems to have determined to show that he too could excel in this type of subject, and sent his *Country blacksmith* to the Academy in 1807. It demonstrates his sympathy with working people, and his ability to draw them unaffectedly as vulnerable, sometimes humorous and always believable inhabitants of the real world.

Fishing upon the Blythe-sand, tide setting in

1809   35 × 47 (89 × 119.5)

Turner showed this modest canvas at his own gallery in 1809 and 1810; he also sent it to the Academy in 1815. It is one of the series of views in the Thames estuary that he produced in the first decade of the century, and establishes a vocabulary of simple, unemphatic compositions and delicately counterpointed forms that Turner was to develop further in the 'Dutch' marines of his later career: 'Van Tromp returning after the Battle off the Dogger Bank', shown in 1833, is to be seen in the same room.

England: Richmond Hill, on the Prince Regent's birthday

1819 $70\frac{7}{8}$ × $131\frac{3}{4}$ (180 × 334.5)

The sequence of English subjects on which Turner worked in the first two decades of the century reached a climax in this large canvas, shown at the Academy in 1819. In it the pastoral freshness of a famous view over the Thames is united with the sweep of a Claudean idyll and the elegant festivity of one of Watteau's *fêtes champêtres*, which Turner convincingly evokes in varied groups of foreground figures.

Studies and Projects

The density and complexity of the ideas conveyed in all these canvases required careful planning and the discipline of much preliminary work. As a consequence, Turner made preparatory sketches and studies all his life, and these afford a vivid glimpse into his creative processes and working methods. He was a very private, secretive man who rarely permitted intruders into his studio, or even the glance of a friend over his shoulder while sketching. Room 103 is devoted to the more personal and intimate aspects of both man and artist. Here, to begin with, is his self-portrait, painted about the time he was elected Associate of the Academy in late 1799, and imitating the dignified, Rembrandtian portrait style of two successful colleagues, John Opie and John Hoppner. Here too are his paints, palettes and brushes, the model ships for which he painted backgrounds, letters and other documents of his life and friendships. The lectures that he gave as Professor of Perspective at the Royal Academy were prepared in sheaves of notes, drafts and transcriptions; the text of one lecture is on display, as are some of his draft verses and poems.

The earliest sketches in the room are those done in the open air on the Thames during the early years of the new century. They are of a freshness and spontaneity that bespeak Turner's long experience of watercolour, and demonstrate his willingness to tackle any mode of expression, any technical challenge. In terms of the developments in continental landscape painting during the rest of the century they are among his most prophetic works. The large study on canvas of 'Willows beside a stream' is unusual in concentrating on a narrow field of vision in which the habits of growth of the trees themselves are the only subject. Turner more commonly incorporated his observations from nature into fully-evolved compositions, often ready for direct transfer from sketchbook or canvas to the final support. Although the Thames sketches in general constitute an exception to this rule, some, like the view of 'The Thames near Walton' or the 'House beside a river', possess a resolved dignity and refinement of design which belies the apparent spontaneity of their execution.

In general he did not favour open-air sketching in oil. He preferred to get down the essential facts of what he saw in pencil in his sketchbooks, and develop his pictures from these at leisure in the studio. Large-scale oil sketches used in the planning of new compositions, together with unfinished

Shipping at the mouth of the Thames
c. 1806–7 (detail)

works, form a majority of the canvases in the Turner Bequest. The most splendid here are the large view of a fortress on a river, probably Namur on the Meuse, which shows us how the finished views of 'Dieppe' and 'Cologne', exhibited in 1825 and 1826 and now in the Frick Collection, New York, would have looked in the course of their execution; and the shimmering Italian subject, probably Civita di Bagnoregio, brushed in during Turner's second visit to Italy in 1828. That visit was out of the ordinary in several respects, not least because Turner actually set up a studio while he was in Rome and exhibited some of the pictures he painted there; and also because he produced a large number of sketches in oil in which he sought to capture the atmosphere of the Italian landscape. The view of Civita di Bagnoregio is very large, suggesting that it might have been worked up into a finished picture perhaps along the lines of the 'Palestrina' (see room 104). Other studies from the Roman stay can be seen in room 106.

A picture closer to completion, if not actually finished, is the lively and somewhat Hogarthian interior subject showing 'George IV at St Giles's, Edinburgh', painted after the King's visit to Scotland in 1822, which prompted Turner to make the journey as well and plan a series of canvases depicting incidents from the royal progress. He seems to have hoped to have the set engraved, but the other subjects, like the 'Provost's Banquet, Edinburgh', were only begun and the scheme came to nothing. The elaborate study for 'The Battle of Trafalgar', on the other hand, did lead to a finished picture, painted for the King in 1822–4. The huge canvas was hung at St James's Palace, but did not find royal favour, and was quickly banished to the Naval Hospital at Greenwich where it remains to this day. This was Turner's first and only royal commission.

Other aspects of the relationship between Turner's sketches and studies and his finished work can be pursued in room 105, where exhibited Venetian pictures are hung opposite preparatory lay-ins; and in room 101, where among the late finished subjects are to be found examples of the expansive atmospheric studies that Turner made in large numbers in the latter part of his career. Many more can be seen in the three reserve galleries on the third floor, where the paintings of the Turner Bequest are displayed in roughly chronological order. These sequences illustrate Turner's extraordinarily varied and imaginative approach to the process of painting, his willingness to experiment with almost any conceivable technique and on any scale.

Although Turner was passionately concerned to preserve his pictures for the national collections he was paradoxically casual about the conditions in which they were kept in his London house, and many, especially the sketches, were permitted to deteriorate badly. Some, as will be seen in the reserve galleries, were never more than the roughest commencements of pictures, and some are, inevitably, unexhibitable except as specimens of rejected essays. But just as he felt that his finished pictures needed to be seen together in order to convey the full breadth and depth of his genius, so today we regard even the most neglected scraps from his studio floor as affording some insight into the working of his mind.

A fortress on the Meuse

c. 1828   68 × 88 (172.5 × 223.5)

In the 1820s Turner painted fewer English subjects, but produced a series of large views of Continental towns, glowing with the warm colour of the Dutchmen Cuyp and Both. This unfinished example probably shows Vauban's great fortress at Namur on the Meuse, which is typically surrounded by the bustling activity of the town and its harbour. The shift of Turner's palette from the muted greys and greens of, say, 'Shipping at the Mouth of the Thames' to a much richer, more highly keyed range of warm blue, yellow and red is strikingly illustrated here.

Tree-tops and sky, Guildford Castle

c. 1807 $10\frac{7}{8}$ × 29 (27.5 × 73.5)

The group of open air studies on panel which Turner executed from a boat on the rivers Thames and Wey in about 1805–10 are among his most spontaneous works. Their fresh naturalism anticipates that of John Constable, and they lack almost all the formal and theoretical qualities that, as a rule, Turner could not help bringing even to his most rapid studies.

Shipping at the mouth of the Thames

c. 1806–7 $33\frac{3}{4} \times 46$ (86×117)

This is an unfinished lay-in for one of the series of scenes in the Thames estuary that Turner painted in the early part of the century. Its simplified plan of muted colours illustrates his method of building up a composition on a structure of subtly harmonised colour masses. An example of a finished work of the same type is 'Fishing upon the Blythe-sand' (see room 108).

Italian Landscape, probably Civita di Bagnoregio

1828 $59 \times 98\frac{1}{4}$ (150×249.5)

The steady lightening of Turner's palette in the middle years of his career was given additional impetus by his two visits to Italy, in 1819 and 1828. On the second, he actually painted a number of pictures in Rome, and seems to have begun several more, including this large and shimmering landscape, one of the most evocative of all his views of central Italy.

The Classical Ideal

The theme of Classical legend that had been inaugurated with the mythological subjects of 1800–1805 was continued in several large canvases of the 1810s. 'The Decline of the Carthaginian Empire' of 1817 is a golden sequel to the silvery 'Dido and Aeneas' of 1814, and to 'Dido building Carthage' which Turner was later to bequeath to the National Gallery as a pendant to Claude's 'Embarkation of the Queen of Sheba'. The importance of Claude at this time is signalled in an even more obvious way by 'Apullia in search of Appullus', exhibited in 1814, which is modelled closely on the Claude 'Landscape with Jacob and Laban' in Lord Egremont's collection. A more personal fusion of classic and topographic elements within the Claudean framework distinguishes the upright canvas of 'Crossing the brook', shown in 1815. Here, with his two daughters as models, Turner reinterprets the countryside of Devon, the home of his father's family, which he had visited in 1811 and 1813, as an idealised landscape suffused with the delicate light of Claude's tenderest inventions.

His first-hand experience of Italy reinforced his admiration for Claude, though by the 1820s his own Claudean style had become a distinct and powerful idiom for the discussion of ideal landscape. Many of the studies that he made in Rome in 1828 rely on a basically Claudean framework, reiterating classic patterns of great beauty, and suffused with a new refulgence of light and colour, as in the beautiful study of 'Lake Nemi' with its broadly indicated masses and marvellously deft placing of a white highlight in the foreground – the ultimate reduction of Claude's ideal to a formal abstraction.

The Decline of the Carthaginian Empire
1817 (detail)

Dido and Aeneas

1814 $57\frac{1}{2} \times 93\frac{3}{8}$ (146 × 237)

Turner's first picture on a theme that was to occupy him throughout his life, this work appeared at the Academy in 1814, with a quotation from the poem that he used as his source, Virgil's *Æneid* in Dryden's translation:

> When next the sun his rising light displays,
> And gilds the world below with purple rays,
> The Queen, Æneas, and the Tyrian Court,
> Shall to the shady woods for sylvan games resort.

The light-hearted pastoral episode is treated in a full-blown Claudean manner, with a range of exquisite effects of light, especially in the distance crowded with buildings and ships, all newly revealed by recent cleaning.

The Decline of the Carthaginian Empire

1817 67 × 94 (170 × 238.5)

This canvas, exhibited in 1817, was designated in Turner's first will to hang in the National Gallery as a pair to his 'Dido building Carthage' of 1815, though he later substituted 'Sun rising through vapour' of 1807. The two Carthage subjects, then, may be read together as comments on the rise and fall of civilisation, sunrise contrasted symbolically with sunset. Turner added the following explanation to his title: 'Rome being determined on the overthrow of her hated rival, demanded from her such terms as might either force her into war or ruin her by compliance: the enervated Carthaginians, in their anxiety for peace, consented to give up even their arms and their children.' Some verses by the artist appeared in the catalogue as well:

> . . . At Hope's delusive smile,
> The chieftain's safety and the mother's pride,
> Were to th'insidious conqu'ror's grasp resign'd;
> While o'er the western wave th'ensanguin'd sun,
> In gathering haze a stormy signal spread,
> And set portentous.

Crossing the brook

1815   76 × 65 (193 × 165)

In this canvas of 1815 Turner created for the first time a large Claudean landscape with a specific English reference. The view is in the valley of the Tamar on the border of Cornwall and Devon, and the silvery light of the heroic *Dido and Æneas* of the previous year is now transformed into that of an English summer day. This is a development of Richard Wilson's practice in many of his English landscape subjects. The two girls in the foreground are said to be portraits of Turner's daughters, Evelina and Georgiana.

Sketch for 'Ulysses deriding Polyphemus'

?1828 $23\frac{5}{8} \times 35\frac{1}{8}$ (60 × 89.2)

One of the large number of oil sketches that Turner painted
while he was in Rome in 1828, this is the only example that can
be related directly to an exhibited work. It adumbrates many of
the essentials of the great painting (on view in Room 104) that
he was to show at the Academy in 1829, though in a subdued
range of colour which hardly prepares us for the brilliant palette
of the picture itself.

Lake Nemi

1828 $23\frac{3}{4} \times 39\frac{1}{4}$ (60.5 × 99.5)

From of a group of studies originally on a single large canvas,
apparently executed during Turner's stay in Rome in 1828. It is
a generalised sketch for the composition of a picture like, say,
'Palestrina' or 'Childe Harold's pilgrimage' (see room 104), but
was never used for a finished work. Indeed it seems to be an
epitome of the 'abstract' classical landscape that underlies so
much of Turner's work in this vein. The highlight of blue and
white in the foreground seems to be of purely formal
significance.

Italy and Antiquity

Although Turner did not visit Italy until 1819 when he was forty-four, the art and landscape of that country had always exerted a special fascination for him. Rome, Florence and Venice were, of course, treasure-houses of art which every serious painter needed to know; in addition, for a landscape painter, the idealised Italian scenery of Claude's and Poussin's pictures had become an inescapable standard by which all landscape was judged, and by which Turner certainly judged his own work almost from the outset of his career. Long before he crossed the Alps he had produced canvases redolent of those masters; so much so that his colleague Sir Thomas Lawrence could write: 'Turner should come to Rome . . . He has an elegance, and often a greatness of invention, that wants a scene like this for its free expansion; whilst the subtle harmony of this atmosphere . . . can only be rendered, according to my belief, by the beauty of his tones . . . It is a fact, that the country and scenes around me, *do* thus impress themselves upon me; and that Turner is always associated with them . . .'.

The influence of Claude's vision of landscape can be felt in Turner's work to the end of his life. Italy, therefore, and the ideal landscape that it inspired, takes a central place in his art, which seems to be epitomised by some of the golden Italian views of his mid-career. Accordingly, the long central room of the Clore Gallery is devoted to a survey of Turner's Italian landscapes, from the ambitious but rather overawed 'Rome from the Vatican' that he painted in 1820 immediately after his first visit, to the more generalised homage of 'Childe Harold's Pilgrimage – Italy' of 1832. The first is an elaborate tribute to Raphael, archetype of the Renaissance genius; the second an 'illustration' of the famous poem by Byron, the epitome of Romanticism.

Byron was preoccupied by the paradox of Italy's physical beauty coexistent with its cultural decline, and Turner quoted verses from 'Childe Harold' to bring out the point. A recurrent theme of several of his Italian subjects is the contrast between beauty and decay, grandeur and decline: both 'The Bay of Baiae' (1823) and 'The Golden Bough' (1834; in reserve collection) speak of the horrors of death and decay in a context of sunlit luxuriance. There is a further comparison of past and present in the beautiful canvas of 'Palestrina' which depicts a place celebrated by Virgil and associated by Turner, in the verses he printed in the catalogue when the

Palestrina
1828 (detail)

picture was shown in London, with Hannibal who

> from yon mural rock, high-crowned Præneste,
> . . . marked, with eagle-eye, Rome as his victim.

One of the works that Turner exhibited in Rome during his second visit there in 1828 was the 'View of Orvieto' which he showed again in London, after some reworking, in 1830.

Another picture to be retouched, and spectacularly, was the 'Regulus' which appeared at the British Institution's exhibition in 1837. By this date Turner had adopted the practice of working extensively on his canvases after they had been hung on the exhibition walls. His colleagues watched in amazement as he proceeded to bring a subject into being often from a practically blank white ground: it was a virtuoso performance, a *tour de force* by which, it has been suggested, Turner sought to instil some of the principles of his art into others. In practice, the exercise only contributed to the mystery that enveloped Turner's creative processes. 'Regulus' was presumably a fully articulated subject before it arrived in London from Rome; yet, for its exhibition at the British Institution, Turner seems to have reduced it to a primeval chaos of colour, out of which he set about recreating the work. 'The picture was a mass of red and yellow of all varieties. Every object was in this fiery state . . . The sun . . . was in the centre; from it were drawn – ruled – lines to mark the rays . . . The picture gradually became wonderfully effective. Just the effect of brilliant sunlight absorbing everything and throwing a misty haze over every object.'

The room is dominated by one of the masterpieces from the National Gallery, 'Ulysses deriding Polyphemus', of 1829, a work described by Ruskin as 'the *central picture* in Turner's career'. This expansive and richly coloured canvas seems to sum up the chromatic experiments of the decade, and brings together all his feeling for the ancient world and for the wonders of nature. A sketch for the picture is to be seen in room 106.

Ulysses deriding Polyphemus

1829 $52\frac{1}{4} \times 80$ (132.7 × 203.2)

If Turner's 1819 visit to Rome caused him to look back to the
Renaissance and the achievements of Raphael, his second stay in
the city seems to have left him freer to indulge his imagination
on the theme of classical legends and stories. Although not an
Italian subject, this great canvas, produced just after his return
to London in 1829 and illustrating a famous passage from
Homer's 'Odyssey', is a meditation on the significance of the
civilisations of the ancient Mediterranean, and the enduring
force of their myths. The dreamlike vision of hero and giant
calling through the crystalline atmosphere of eternal morning in
the silent presence of all the elements – earth, sun, fire and water
are witnesses to the struggle – is one of the most intense and
moving of all Turner's evocations of the ancient world.

Rome from the Vatican. Raffaelle accompanied by
La Fornarina, preparing his pictures for the decoration
of the Loggia

1820 $69\frac{3}{4} \times 132$ (177×335.3)

Turner's first response to his visit to Italy in 1819 was to paint
this huge canvas, the only one he finished for the Academy the
following spring. It is a complete survey of all that he had learnt
in Rome, a comprehensive panorama of the city from the
decorations of the Vatican at its heart to the mountains of the
Abruzzi which encircle it. Raphael, one of the greatest geniuses
of the Renaissance, becomes a focus for Turner's meditations on
the role of the artist in society. The objects arranged in the
foreground include sculpture, a landscape painting, a portrait
and architectural plans, perhaps alluding as much to Turner's
own creativity as to Raphael's.

Forum Romanum

1826 $57\frac{3}{8} \times 93$ (145.7×236.2)

Turner planned this, the third great canvas to result from his
first visit to Italy, as a contribution to the collection of the
architect Sir John Soane. His use of a segmental arch to frame
the top of the composition may even be a deliberate echo of the
segmental ceilings in Soane's house. The dense accumulation of
architectural detail in the picture is equally a tribute to Soane's
profession and to the fantastic drawings issued by his studio to
illustrate his ideas. The subject, with its concentration on motifs
taken from the ruins of ancient Rome, complements Turner's
reflections on the high Renaissance in 'Rome from the Vatican'.

The Bay of Baiae, with Apollo and the Sibyl

1823 $57\frac{1}{4} \times 94$ (145.5×239)

After Turner's visit to Italy in 1819 it was some years before he
again tackled the kinds of ideal Mediterranean landscape at
which he had excelled in the previous decade. 'The Bay of
Baiae', exhibited in 1823, was his first essay of this type
undertaken in the light of first-hand experience and marks a
smooth and uninterrupted continuity with the earlier works in
the same vein. It is as much as ever an imaginative reinterpretation of Italy; a colleague wrote on the frame when the
picture was first shown 'Splendide Mendax' – 'A glorious lie'.
The inherent transience of all physical beauty, however, is very
much a part of Turner's picture: the Sibyl accepts Apollo's gift
of as many years of life as she holds grains of sand, but without
eternal youth lives on for an infinity of time, wasting away to
become a disembodied voice.

View of Orvieto

1828; reworked 1830 $36 \times 48\frac{1}{2}$ (91×123)

One of the pictures painted during Turner's stay in Rome in
1828, this gentle landscape approaches more closely to the
topography of a particular spot than any of the others, and seems
to be based on sketches made round Orvieto on the journey to
Rome. It is nevertheless a highly romanticised view, and blends
the Claudean ideal and the needs of topography in a character-
istically poetic way unique to Turner.

Regulus

1828; reworked 1837 $35\frac{1}{4} \times 48\frac{3}{4}$ (91 × 124)

A picture painted in Rome in 1828 which Turner retouched for exhibition at the British Institution in London in 1837, this is another adaptation of the Claudean model of the Seaport. Regulus, a Roman general captured by the Carthaginians, is sent back to Rome to negotiate a treaty, which he will refuse to do. Returned to Carthage, he will be tortured by having his eyelids cut off, so that the sun blinds him. The picture as repainted in 1837 gave 'the effect of brilliant sunlight absorbing everything and throwing a misty haze over every object' as an observer described it, and seems to have been intended to present Regulus's fate in vivid actuality.

Childe Harold's pilgrimage – Italy

1832 $56 \times 97\frac{3}{4}$ (142 × 248)

Like the 'Bay of Baiae' this picture celebrates the beauty of Italy, which endures even after the decay of the civilisation that made the country great. The scene is imaginary – a composition of many ideal Italian elements – and was shown at the Academy with lines from the poem by Byron referred to in the title:

> . . . and now, fair Italy!
> Thou art the garden of the world.
> Even in thy desert what is like to thee?
> Thy very weeds are beautiful, thy waste
> More rich than other climes' fertility . . .

ROOM 102

*Petworth and
East Cowes*

His preoccupation with colour and light is characteristic of the second half of Turner's career. The gloomy grandeur of mountains or stormy seas which had inspired his weightiest statements hitherto is replaced by the equally sublime brilliance of the sun, invading every aspect of reality and disintegrating it under our eyes. But in his journey to this final view of the world, Turner made further excursions, as a necessary corollary, into the language of chiaroscuro – the interplay of strong light with powerful shadow. In these essays he looked back, of course, to the example of Rembrandt, whose work he consciously imitated in subjects like 'Pilate washing his hands' of 1830. His renewed interest in interior scenes, associated as it is with these experiments with light and shade, found a channel in a series of studies of the houses of his patrons, two of which in particular yielded him inspiration of a special order.

East Cowes Castle, on the Isle of Wight, was the home of the successful architect John Nash, and here Turner was able to explore the possibilities not only of a romantic mock-castle on a bluff above the sea, but the exciting atmosphere of the Cowes regatta. His sketches of the boats leaving their moorings, or, later, beating to windward, with the castle in the distance behind them, are for pictures exhibited in 1828 (and now in other collections) which are pervaded by the sparkling summer light and exhilaration of the occasion. The sketch of an interior at East Cowes with a music party, however, is richly shadowed and Rembrandtian in its colouring, while the historical fantasy of 'Boccaccio relating the tale of the Birdcage' (also shown in 1828) transforms the reality of East Cowes Castle into a medieval dream modelled, once again, on Watteau, though this time through the intermediary influence of an admired contemporary, Thomas Stothard. It may have been in the company of Nash that he was inspired to make a series of studies on architectural themes – the canvases now known as 'A vaulted hall' (in reserve collection) and 'Interior at Petworth' are examples, sonorous with Rembrandtian light and shade in settings that remind us of the fantasies of Piranesi.

Petworth, in Sussex, was the other house in which Turner found an important stimulus for his work. The easy-going third Earl of Egremont was a keen collector of modern British art and host to numerous painters and sculptors, giving them facilities for working on the spot and encouraging

*Chichester Canal
c. 1828 (detail)*

them to take part in the multifarious life of his household. He had bought his first picture from Turner in 1801, and in about 1827 commissioned him to paint a group of panels for the decoration of the Dining Room. Turner produced two sets of scenes at or near Petworth: one set is still at the house, the other, including the tranquil evening landscapes of 'Chichester Canal', and 'Petworth Park: Tillington Church in the distance', was in the artist's studio at his death and now forms the centrepiece of Room 102. Petworth's old masters included many important Van Dycks, and Turner paid tribute to that artist in some of his work done at the house. The 'Lady in Van Dyck Costume' imitates such pictures as Van Dyck's portrait of 'Anne, Lady Rich', and demonstrates Turner's powers as a painter of soft and luminous flesh. In general the composition resembles his 'Jessica' shown at the Academy in 1830 and still at Petworth. An important corollary of all these pictures is the long series of studies that he made on small sheets of blue paper, in bright watercolour and bodycolour, of life in and around the house. These are still in the Turner Bequest.

While he was working with renewed interest on the theme of the interior, Turner's attitudes to what happens out of doors were broadening and deepening; his understanding of light as the medium in which everything exists and is perceived became the dominant motive of his landscape paintings, and he sought out ever more spacious scenery in which to explore the effects that most fascinated him. His later years saw the production of mountain subjects and seascapes from which many of the formal and chromatic characteristics of his earlier work seem to have been banished altogether, so that they are studies in pure light and atmosphere – the true essence of nature. Subjects that had previously been beyond the reach of any painter were opened up to him; and scenes that had been the object of other artists' attention were taken over and endowed with fresh life and meaning.

Pilate washing his hands

1830   36 × 48 (91.5 × 122)

Among the many artists who stimulated Turner to emulation
in the years about 1830 (when this canvas appeared at the
Academy) Rembrandt was one he had already learned much
from in his youth. It is surprising that he should have embarked
on so elaborate a pastiche as this in his maturity. He may have
been spurred on by the Rembrandtian compositions of his friend
and fellow-Academician, George Jones. Another Biblical
subject, 'The Burning Fiery Furnace', shown in 1832 and also
exhibited here, was executed in friendly but explicit rivalry with
Jones and again seems to imitate his manner.

Petworth Park : Tillington Church in the distance

c. 1828 $25\frac{3}{8} \times 57\frac{3}{8}$ (64.5 × 145.5)

The view from the south front of Petworth House across the park
was one that Turner drew many times, and there are several
bodycolour studies of sunsets taken from the same spot.
Although this picture seems to have originally hung at Petworth
it was replaced by the version there today, showing a cricket
match and stags fighting. In the Turner Bequest picture the
atmosphere is more tranquil, with quietly grazing deer and the
figure of Lord Egremont himself striding across the turf, while
his dogs rush out to greet him.

Chichester Canal

c. 1828 $25\frac{3}{4} \times 53$ (65.5 × 134.5)

Among the pictures painted for the dining room at Petworth is a
view of Chichester Canal, for which this exquisite study was a
preparation. It is broadly yet delicately handled, with passages
resembling watercolour. Lord Egremont had a financial interest
in the canal, which Turner acknowledges in his image of the ship
on its glassy water; but the spirit of the picture is far removed
from the world of trade or commerce: it is one of the most
tranquilly serene of all his landscapes.

Music at East Cowes Castle
c. 1835 $47\frac{3}{4} \times 35\frac{5}{8}$ (121 × 90.5)
One of the most celebrated images in Turner's output, this
enigmatic interior peopled by figures in fancy dress has recently
been found to show a room at East Cowes, and, since his hostess
there, Mrs John Nash, was an accomplished pianist it is likely
that it records a music party attended by the artist and perhaps
shows her at the piano. Like other unfinished works of the period
– it probably dates from the early 1830s – it is, however, difficult
to interpret and is best appreciated as a private fantasy of the
artist's.

A Ship Aground

1828 $27\frac{1}{2} \times 53\frac{1}{2}$ (69.8 × 135.9)

Although this canvas is the same size and shape as the series of
compositions that Turner made for the dining-room at Petworth
its subject-matter is less obviously connected with Lord
Egremont. It is nevertheless a very beautiful and economical
evocation of the sea, perhaps designed as a pendant to the view
of 'Brighton Chain Pier', for which a sketch is also in Room 102.
The composition was used in modified form for a finished picture
exhibited in 1831, 'Fort Vimieux' (private collection).

Between Decks

1827 $12 \times 19\frac{1}{8}$ (30.5 × 48.6)

While he was staying at East Cowes Castle in 1827 Turner sent
to London for two rolls of canvas, on which he painted a number
of studies of shipping at the Cowes Regatta, a sporting event that
had only recently been introduced. Among the sketches was this
intimate study of sailors and their visiting sweethearts aboard a
man of war anchored off Cowes. It has been suggested that
Turner used the ship as a base from which he made all these
open-air sketches. There are two finished pictures of the
Regatta, both exhibited in 1828. One is now in the Victoria and
Albert Museum, the other in Indianapolis.

Venice

A case in point is Venice. Turner had made very few views of Venice as a result of his visit there in 1819 – some beautiful wash studies and two finished watercolours are almost all we have, apart from the pencil notes that he kept in sketchbooks. But in 1833 he showed at the Academy a picture of the 'Bridge of Sighs, Ducal Palace and Custom-house, Venice: Canaletti painting' which announced a new range of works, and the source of Turner's inspiration for them. For the next decade and a half he painted Venetian subjects of ever-increasing airiness and luminosity, which owe their origin as much to Turner's consciousness of Canaletto's achievement as they do to his response to Venice itself as a city of vast, shimmering spaces enlivened by shining water and marble, perfectly suited to his pre-occupations. These subjects were popular with his patrons, as they were with his imitators and forgers after his death; but the Bequest includes a series of fine examples, which are displayed in a room of their own. The sequence presents in microcosm the system of painting that Turner evolved, under the influence of his own watercolour technique, of rendering objects in finely applied and brilliant local colour on a white ground which shines luminously through each subject. One of the most richly detailed, with elaborately drawn architecture, is 'Venice, the Bridge of Sighs' of 1840; while 'The Sun of Venice going to sea' of 1843 borrows the subject, and something of the handling, of one of the numerous water-colours that he made in Venice at the time of his last visit there in 1840. As the years pass, Turner's Venice sinks ever deeper into its envelope of white mist, until buildings and inhabitants are merged into the general radiance.

Yet there persists a clear distinction between the exhibited subjects, like 'Evening, going to the ball', or its pendant 'Morning, returning from the ball, St. Martino' of 1845, and the pale, almost featureless lay-ins that survive from the studio, and which were to be worked up on the Academy's walls. There are several of these in the Turner Bequest and they are displayed here, for a few months only, without frames in order to draw attention to the important differences between what were for Turner merely beginnings and the complex, elaborate statements of his finished pictures. Although his increasing preoccupation with light and atmosphere in the last years of his career brings the two stages closer, they are nonetheless distinct. The beginnings cannot be interpreted in terms of this

The Dogano, San Giorgio, Citella, from the steps of the Europa
1842 (detail)

subject matter as they were never meant to be 'read' by the public. On the other hand, Turner emphasised the rich content of the exhibited pictures by giving them titles full of specific reference. His intention, even in these his most hazily atmospheric works, is still to remind us that the wonders of nature are significant only as the context in which human life is lived.

Bridge of Sighs, Ducal Palace and Custom-house, Venice :
Canaletti painting

1833 $20\frac{3}{16} \times 32\frac{7}{16}$ (51×82.5)

As with other subjects and places, Turner seems to have required
the stimulus of art in order to engage fully with the reality of
Venice. This, his first view in oils of the city, appeared at the
Academy in 1833 just before his second visit, and so more than a
decade since he had been there. It is indeed less a response to
Venice itself than an act of homage to the greatest of Venice's
view-painters, Canaletto. The *vedutista* appears in the left-hand
corner, at work on a framed picture on an easel; the serene,
resonant blue of the sky and the four-square presentation of the
architectural subject indicate that Turner had Canaletto's own
work very much in mind.

Venice, the Bridge of Sighs

1840   24 × 36 (61 × 91.5)

Like his Venetian view of 1833 with 'Canaletti painting', this
picture, exhibited in 1840, seems to owe something of its
brilliance of colour and firmness of organisation to the
eighteenth-century master, though in its assured drawing of the
architecture and elaborately invented foreground groups it is
typical of Turner. The atmospheric haze which gently dissolves
the forms of the buildings announces the vaporous atmosphere of
the Venetian views which were to follow. Some lines from
Byron's *Childe Harold* appeared with the title in the Academy
Catalogue,

> I stood upon a bridge, a palace and a prison
> on each hand

alluding to the Doge's palace and the prison on either side of the
Bridge of Sighs.

*The Dogano, San Giorgio, Citella, from the steps of the
Europa*

1842   24¼ × 36½ (62 × 92.5)

This picture was exhibited at the Academy in 1842 and bought
by Robert Vernon who bequeathed his collection to the
National Gallery – an important impulse behind Turner's
arrangements for the disposal of his own works. Vernon's picture
was, indeed, the first by Turner to hang in the National Gallery.
It shows the view from the steps of the artist's hotel at the mouth
of the Grand Canal. The influence of Canaletto can still be felt;
it was to disappear from the Venetian subjects of the following
year.

The Sun of Venice going to Sea

1843 $24\frac{1}{4} \times 36\frac{1}{4}$ (61.5 × 92)

Exhibited in 1843, this picture marks a departure from the Canaletto-inspired Venetian pictures that Turner had painted hitherto. It is blonder in tonality and freer in handling, being treated almost as a watercolour, with fine strokes of bright colour on a background almost white. A watercolour study related to the subject exists, in the National Gallery of Scotland, Vaughan Bequest.

Morning, returning from the ball, St. Martino

1845 $24\frac{1}{2} \times 36\frac{1}{2}$ (62 × 92.5)

A view of Venice in which the architecture and the life of the city have become immersed in the all-enveloping mist of light and atmosphere that pervades Turner's work of his last years. This picture was shown at the Academy in 1845, one of a pair – the other is 'Venice, evening, going to the ball'. His last Venetian subjects were exhibited in the following year.

These are the themes that animate the paintings of his last years. The final room in the main suite is devoted to masterpieces of the decade or so preceding Turner's death in 1851, both exhibited pictures and studies. The former illustrate his continuing concern with the serious issues of human existence, while the latter pursue the fascination with effects of light and atmosphere that had governed his perception of nature all his life. The long series of atmospheric studies that he produced at this time, of which 'Yacht approaching the coast' and 'Sunrise with sea-monsters' are particularly developed examples, provide a background of generalised emotion from which the more specific subjects of the exhibited works emerge.

Those works take a remarkable variety of forms. Some of the largest and grandest, like the 'Opening of the Wallhalla' (1843), continue Turner's long-established preoccupation with crowded landscapes contrasting the role of the common man and that of the 'men of destiny' in the great historical events of Europe. In this example, the event is a contemporary one, and the verses that Turner composed to accompany it make it clear that the canvas commemorates jointly the victory of Liberty over the tyranny of Napoleon, and that of the peaceful arts over the barbarism of war. Looking back along the central gallery we are reminded of Napoleon's defeat in the shadowy 'Field of Waterloo' at the far end of the vista. The contrast emphasises the often repeated theme of Turner's late years, the triumph of light over darkness, and reflects the steady progress of his own art from the sombre tonality of his early work to the luminous brilliance of his last canvases. In the 1840s Turner sometimes chose to set out such oppositions in paired works, rather than in single compositions; a similar theme to that of the 'Wallhalla' motivates the couple entitled 'Peace. Burial at sea' and 'War. The exile and the rock limpet' of 1842, where the regrets of the fallen and exiled Napoleon are set against the obsequies of an admired brother artist, Sir David Wilkie.

The square, octagonal or circular format of these paired pictures marks a culmination of Turner's fascination with the vortex, the whirling spiral of energy that defines the depth of the picture-space and binds all life and nature within it in a single dynamic movement. Perhaps the climax of the series is the pair titled 'Shade and darkness. The evening of the deluge' and 'Light and colour (Goethe's theory). The morning after the deluge. Moses

Norham Castle
c. 1845–50 (detail)

writing the book of Genesis'. These were exhibited in 1843, and may have been prompted by the appearance in 1840 of the large 'Deluge' by Francis Danby that now hangs in the Tate Gallery, and which attempts some of the effects Turner himself had already essayed in his own early 'Deluge' picture of about 1805 and in 'Hannibal crossing the Alps'. The format he chooses is, however, deliberately restricted to the compact, vertical square, into which he packs enough of power and energy to fill a much larger painting. The reference to Goethe reminds us of the German author's proposal that colours carry with them emotional connotations, varying from joy to despair, corresponding to their respective warmth or coolness; and indeed the two works exploit the contrasts of cold and hot, dark and light, horror and exultation with a theatrical force that seems to sum up the whole range of Turner's art.

Such a broad gamut of emotional reference, always a vital feature of his work, is never more pronounced than in these late canvases, which are far from being simply exercises in the depiction of climatic conditions. The theme of human suffering in the context of natural upheaval is pursued to new heights of technical and expressive imagination in the famous 'Snow storm – steam-boat off a harbour's mouth making signals in shallow water, and going by the lead' of 1842. The careful precision of this title warns us that this is no generalised evocation of sea and storm: a quite specific event is taking place, and Turner emphasises the fact by adding to his title the information that 'The author was in this storm on the night the Ariel left Harwich'. Questioned about it later, he said that he had had himself tied to the mast, and did not think he would survive, 'but I felt bound to record it if I did'. Whether these events really occurred or not – and it is possible that Turner invented them – it is clear that he was anxious that his picture, all too easily dismissed by critics of the day as 'soapsuds and whitewash', should be understood as a true account of reality. The details he invents are like the 'facts' presented by a novelist – they reinforce general observations of human experience by creating specific and believable circumstances to which these observations can be related.

Even more explicitly, his very last paintings, shown at the Academy in the year before his death, 1850, stress the unity of nature and humanity. They are a group of four illustrations (of which one is now lost) to Virgil's

Aeneid, concluding a lifetime's interest in the story of Dido's city of Carthage and her fatal love affair with the hero Aeneas who abandoned her to pursue his destiny as the founder of Rome. In taking up this classic story, he also uttered his last statement on the theme of the ideal Claudean landscape: all four pictures are golden harbour scenes of the kind that he had perfected in 'Dido building Carthage' and 'The decline of the Carthaginian Empire'. Now, however, Claude's brilliant sunlight has attained an obliterating power that almost annihilates the scenes of heroic passion that it illumines; both sun and moon are witnesses to the tragedy as it unfolds, and the times of the day provide diverse and quite specific conditions in which it takes place. So Turner's verses from the 'Fallacies of Hope' link each subject with a natural phenomenon, 'Mercury sent to admonish Aeneas' is amplified with these lines:

> Beneath the morning mist,
> Mercury waited to tell him of his neglected fleet.

If Turner in many of his finished works seeks to be a novelist in paint, his sketches are poems of the most exquisite subtlety. His many sea studies can be understood as experiments in preparation for pictures such as 'Fire at Sea' (in reserve gallery) and 'Snow Storm', but other highly atmospheric essays of the 1840s are very different in mood and purpose. The series of compositions based on subjects from his great survey of landscape painting, the 'Liber Studiorum' (published 1807–1819), is often lyrical, contemplative and even transcendental in its concern with the quiet radiance of morning sunlight and solitude. One of these subjects is indeed known as 'Solitude': a haze of diffused brilliance almost obliterates a distant castle and its surrounding trees. Similarly the view of 'Norham Castle, sunrise', which takes up one of Turner's favourite subjects, is dissolved into a prismatic radiance of red, yellow and blue.

*The Fighting 'Temeraire' tugged to her last berth to be
broken up, 1838*

Exh. 1839 $35\frac{1}{4} \times 48$ (91 × 122)

This picture has been regarded as an image of peculiar
importance in Turner's output ever since it was exhibited at the
Academy in 1839. The artist himself had a special regard for it,
and once referred to it as 'My Darling.' He had seen the old
warship, a veteran of Trafalgar, against a sunset sky on the
Thames, pulled to the breakers' yard by a small sooty tug. Like
the railway train in 'Rain, Steam, and Speed' the tug is a vivid
symbol of the modern world, and Turner seems to lament not
only the passing of the old order of sailing-ships that he had so
long loved to paint, but also his own decline into old age. The
picture is a gentle and at the same time noble elegy for a long
and fruitful life drawing to its predestined close.

Sunrise with sea monsters

c. 1845   36 × 48 (91.5 × 122)

One of the long series of studies which Turner made in his later years, exploring the effects of light on the sea, of storm and wreck, of wind, sky and water. Here his imagination runs freely on the theme of the denizens of the deep, and suggests that the ocean is peopled with sentient and passionate beings just as the earth is. At about the same date he was working on his studies of Whalers, which explore another aspect of the theme.

The Opening of the Wallhalla, 1842

Exh. 1843 $44\frac{5}{16}$ × 79 (112.5 × 200.5)

The 'Walhalla' had been erected by Ludwig of Bavaria above the Danube near Regensburg as a temple in honour of the heroes of Germany's arts and sciences. Turner showed this important picture, painted on a large panel, at the Academy in 1843, and two years later sent it to the Congress of European Art in Munich. It was laughed at and returned, damaged, with £7 to pay for its transport. The reception of the work in Europe was ironic, for in it Turner declared his solidarity with European culture after the barbarism of the Napoleonic Wars. It is a picture about light, civilisation and art, a testament of Turner's ideals and his faith in the future.

The Evening Star

c. 1830 $36\frac{1}{4} \times 48\frac{1}{4}$ (92.1 × 122.6)

This exquisite study seems to date from the early 1830s, and may derive from Turner's experiments with mezzotint in his 'Little Liber Studiorum' series of about 1826. In those he had explored the delicate effects of light at dusk or just after moonrise, making preparatory watercolours which are similar in mood to this tranquil work.

Snow storm – Steam-boat off a harbour's mouth making signals in shallow water, and going by the lead

1842 $57\frac{1}{2} \times 93\frac{1}{2}$ (146 × 237.5)

The careful wording of the title should ensure that we do not mistake this picture, exhibited in 1842, as a mere 'impression' of wild nature. Turner is anxious to assure us that he is reporting a specific event, minutely observed and recorded by means of his technical mastery. The composition, based on a whirling structure of fragmented arcs, is unusual in its freedom from the classical models that underlie even such vividly novel works as 'Rain, Steam, and Speed.'

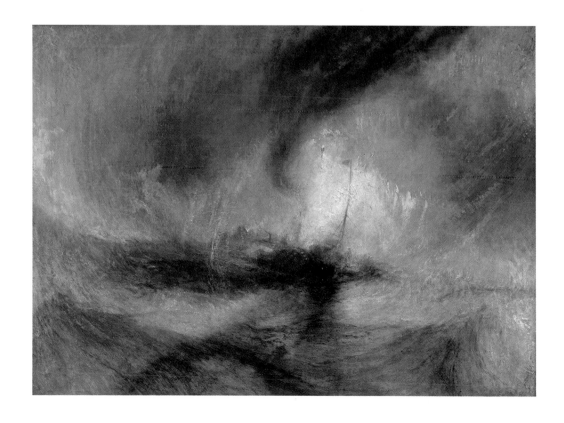

Peace – burial at sea

1842 $34\frac{1}{4} \times 34\frac{1}{8}$ (87×86.5)

Turner's lifelong attachment to the Royal Academy and its
members, and his habit of referring to other artists in his own
work, come together in this commemoration of his old friend and
rival David Wilkie. It was exhibited in 1842; Wilkie had died
suddenly at sea the previous year on his return from the Middle
East and Turner depicts his funeral off Gibraltar as a moment of
profound calm. The black sails of the ship were criticised by a
colleague as untrue to life. 'I only wish I had any colour to make
them blacker', Turner replied.

*Light and colour (Goethe's Theory) – the morning after the
Deluge – Moses writing the book of Genesis*

1843 31×31 (78.5×78.5)

The second of Turner's pair of pictures, shown at the Academy
in 1843 and alluding to Goethe's theory of colours, which
proposed that the cool and warm sides of the spectrum have
their own specific emotional connotations. 'Shade and darkness
– the evening of the Deluge' exploits a palette of blue, grey and
brown while this triumphant burst of light, announcing God's
Covenant with Man after the flood, is couched in a brilliant
range of reds and yellows. The raised serpent in the centre of the
design, alluding to the brazen serpent raised by Moses in the
wilderness as a cure for plague, is a symbol of Christ's redemption
of man in the New Covenant. The religious meaning of the
picture is, however, complicated by Turner's verses, added to
the title in the Academy catalogue. These speak of 'earth's
humid bubbles', brought forth by the 'returning sun' only to
burst 'ephemeral as the summer fly, Which rises, flits, expands,
and dies.'

Rain, Steam, and Speed – the Great Western Railway

1844 $35\frac{3}{4} \times 48$ (91 × 122)

In this extraordinary image the seventy-year-old Turner draws together all the strands of his lifelong concerns for classical art, for light and atmosphere, and for the life of the world in which he lived. The evocation of speed as manifested in that most modern of inventions the steam engine is used to restate in terms of the greatest virtuosity the exhilaration of the open air, while this celebration of a triumphant technological future is poignantly contrasted with the old rural world, presented in the distant ploughman and hare running in front of the train. The whole airy vision is built on the firm structure of one of Poussin's classical landscapes, with strongly marked horizontal and diagonal stresses reinforcing the speed of the train and the measured movement of the eye through palpably evoked space.

Watercolour Room: Works on Paper

The interrelationship between studies and sketches in oil and the finished paintings provides invaluable insights into the working of Turner's mind, and into his creative methods. Those insights are broadened still further by the contents of the sketchbooks and other works on paper which abound in the artist's Bequest. In general, his preparations for paintings in oil were made in monochrome – pencil, pen and ink or chalk – in the sketchbooks; examples of such work are displayed in cases in the main galleries. The evolution of the finished watercolours can be followed in still greater detail, since it was not possible for a watercolour 'lay-in' to be reworked as one in oil could be. Each experimental beginning had to be commenced on a fresh sheet; and as Turner was meticulous in subjecting his elaborate compositions to careful chromatic, structural and tonal analysis he often employed many sheets in sequences of exploratory studies which lead up to a final statement. While the majority of the finished watercolours that he produced all his life were sold to collectors and are now scattered in collections public and private throughout the world, the preparatory studies for them remained for the most part in his studio. They number many hundreds and it would not be possible to display them all simultaneously; but selections of them, with other work on paper, are shown, sometimes in the context of thematic exhibitions, in the Watercolour Room.

The earliest signed and dated drawings are watercolour views of Oxford and its neighbourhood. Soon after Turner had sent in his first submission to the Royal Academy, at the age of fifteen, he had begun to plan a series of topographical views for possible publication, after the fashion of the time – an ambitious scheme that was symptomatic of the energy with which he pursued his first profession. Already by 1793 he was exhibiting works that impressed contemporaries as novel and exceptionally sensitive records of light and climate, and by the time he was twenty his watercolours of cathedrals, abbeys and grand scenery marked him out as the leading exponent of the medium. Two fine finished examples in the Bequest are the 'Llanthony Abbey' and 'Valle Crucis and Dinas Bran' of 1794. His early essays in oil stimulated much technical experimentation with both watercolour and the closely related medium of bodycolour (gouache) and during the late 1790s the progress of his art was dramatic. The impact of a

Shields Lighthouse
*c.*1826 (enlarged detail)

tour to the Welsh mountains in 1798 produced studies of a range, splendour and expressive force unknown in landscape art hitherto; they are often very large, with corresponding depth and richness of colour. In the case of studies like the 'Welsh mountains with an army on the march' of about 1799 they adumbrate elaborate historical subjects intended to be finished in watercolour.

These developments culminated in the series of finished watercolours that he made of Swiss scenes in the years following his visit to the Continent in 1802. The Bequest contains many large chalk drawings made on the spot among the mountains, as well as a grand colour study for a view thought to be in the Pass of St Gotthard, and the finished 'Battle of Fort Rock in the Val d'Aosta', shown at the Academy in 1815 and one of Turner's most complex statements on the interaction of man and nature, in a historical context. While these Sublime subjects were occupying him, Turner was also engaged on various projects to record the buildings and scenery of England, often for private patrons, but frequently for publication as engraved plates in local histories, topographical and travel books, and, in the case of one commission, for the *Oxford Almanack*. By 1806 the range of his subject-matter in watercolour and oil seemed to merit some more widely publicized demonstration, and he began work on the long series of plates published as the *Liber Studiorum*. The monochrome designs that he made for this highly influential work provide a vital insight into his attitudes to his own art during the first half of his career. Further didactic activity of these years was his work as Professor of Perspective at the Royal Academy, for which he prepared a series of six lectures, with illustrations in the form of diagrams and large watercolour drawings. His colleague Thomas Stothard, although quite deaf, regularly attended because, he said, 'there is much to *see* at Turner's lectures'.

In the 1810s two important commissions for watercolours were in hand, the 'Views in Sussex' for John Fuller of Rosehill near Hastings, and the long sequence of 'Picturesque Views on the Southern Coast of England' for the engraver and publisher George Cooke. Although none of the finished subjects are in the Bequest, much of the preparatory work for these projects can be seen, as well as the sketchbooks used during the various tours on which Turner gathered material for them. His growing mastery of all aspects of the depiction of nature is evident in the fluent and highly personal studies in watercolour that he made on the Thames in about 1807, and in the small oil sketches that date from his tour of Devon in 1813. His first visit to Italy in 1819 gave rise to a large quantity of careful records of scenery, architecture, and works of art; and to a long series of colour studies capturing the spirit of Venice, Rome and Naples.

Of a more cerebral nature are the impressive colour studies that he made in the studio as a stage towards the production of the *Southern Coast* designs, or the series of views in the north of England for the *History of Richmondshire*, published between 1818 and 1823, and an extensive series of even more experimental trials which can be associated with the greatest of these topographical watercolour sequences, the *Picturesque Views in England and Wales* on which Turner was working for a decade from 1825. Only one completed design for that work remains in the Bequest, the unpublished 'Merton College, Oxford' of about 1830; but the Tate's own collection also supplies a finished subject, the lovely 'Aldeburgh', which was one of the earliest to be engraved.

But several complete series of finished watercolours were retained by the artist and provide a survey of his output for the engraver during these important years of his career. The richly worked texture, with meticulous technique and brilliant colour, of his mature watercolour style can be seen in the two series of *Rivers* and *Ports of England*, which appeared between 1823 and 1828; these were engraved in mezzotint in two series which seem to have provided the impetus for him to embark on a group of mezzotint plates that he executed himself. The group, known as the 'Little Liber Studiorum', includes some of the most powerful and individual of all romantic prints; they are based on summary, but highly evocative, watercolour sketches in which Turner furnishes himself with the broadest general ideas from which to work.

By this time he was involved in yet further enterprises for the publishers, and many of his tours of the late 1820s and early 1830s were planned to supply material for new projects – the 'Annual Tours' of the Loire and the Seine which were issued in 1833–5, the illustrations to Scott, Rogers and Byron, Milton and the Bible. The 'Annual Tours' were three volumes of a never-completed series surveying the 'Great Rivers of Europe'. Turner travelled far afield collecting subjects for this. As he did at Petworth, he worked on small sheets of blue paper, using the opaque medium of gouache, or bodycolour, to achieve a brilliance and intensity that seems to have been calculated as a direct challenge to his engravers. Similarly, the small-scale illustrations to the poets that he executed in pure watercolour are worked in a meticulous miniaturist's technique which enables Turner to cram a wealth of detail and immense grandeur into tiny, jewel-like designs which often embrace the same sweeping panoramic subject-matter as his larger watercolours.

The translation of his watercolour designs into engraved illustrations – whether in line or mezzotint – was of great importance to him. He supervised with a highly critical eye the successive stages of printmaking, sending back the engravers' proofs with comments and 'touchings' that reveal his penetrating sensitivity. The collections include a representative holding of the prints made after his mature designs, including a number of progress proofs. They indicate the final form which his ideas were intended to take, a form almost bafflingly far removed, in its precision of multitudinous detail rendered in black and white, from the broad colour studies with which he was accustomed to begin the process of creation.

Turner's sketching habits changed somewhat in the later part of his career. From the mid-1820s he had begun to take with him on his Continental tours a new, soft-covered sketchbook which could be rolled up in a greatcoat pocket. These 'roll' sketchbooks never entirely replaced the small notebooks in which he was accustomed to record the scenery and buildings that he encountered; but in the 1830s and '40s he increasingly made use of their more spacious pages to develop rough pencil outlines into more elaborate statements in washes of watercolour, sometimes applied on the journey, though not normally on the spot. These exist in their hundreds, and although many of them were of sufficient completeness to be sold, and have found their way into other collections, a large number remain in the Bequest. They afford a remarkable survey of Turner's activities in his sixties and seventies – as alertly receptive and as original as ever. Some are slight studies, evocative impressions of mountain villages, ravines and lakes; and there is a famous sequence of views in Venice, recording the palaces and churches along the canals, and the continual shift and shimmer of light on the lagoon. Others are more highly worked up; they achieve a wholeness that seems complete in itself. These are often drawings that Turner made as guides to his patrons when they were selecting subjects for finished watercolours; they only hint at his full intentions. The 'sample' studies of the 'Dark Rigi', for instance, or of 'Zurich', seen in a panoramic view, are magnificent tokens of his powers in old age, but must be seen in conjunction with the finished works to be fully understood. Fine examples of these, including the fully realised 'Zurich' of 1842 and the 'Lucerne: moonlight' of 1843, are to be found in the Department of Prints and Drawings of the British Museum, while grandiose late colour studies of mountains and lakes executed on a large scale exist in the corresponding Department of the Victoria and Albert Museum. Both collections contain fine works by Turner of all periods, as do the Drawings Departments of the Ashmolean Museum, Oxford and the Fitzwilliam Museum, Cambridge. Among other important assemblages of Turner's work in Britain are the extensive holdings of the Whitworth Art Gallery and the City Art Gallery in Manchester, and the group of fine examples bequeathed to the National Gallery of Scotland in Edinburgh by Henry Vaughan. Vaughan also left part of his Turner collection to the National Gallery of Ireland in Dublin.

Many of Turner's greatest paintings and watercolours are scattered widely outside Britain, most notably in the United States. The National Gallery of Art in Washington, the Frick Collection in New York and the Museums of Philadelphia and Boston all possess fine examples; and the Yale Center for British Art at New Haven, Connecticut, holds the largest Turner collection outside London. The artist's output in watercolour was so extensive that there still remain numerous examples in private hands, and they frequently appear on the market. The oil paintings have nearly all reached public collections although a few are still in private ownership; they come on to the market only rarely. It is a testimony to the prodigious creativity of Turner that unknown works by him, sometimes of superb quality, occasionally come to light even today. The Clore Gallery, therefore, is far from being the only repository of Turner's work; but as the home of the Turner Bequest it is a natural centre for the study and enjoyment of his achievement as a whole.

Valle Crucis and Dinas Bran

1794–5 $18\frac{1}{4} \times 14\frac{7}{8}$ (464 × 377)

An extensive tour of the Midland counties and part of north
Wales in 1794 supplied Turner with a wealth of new subject-
matter. The ruins of Valle Crucis Abbey near Llangollen in the
romantic valley of the Dee were a popular theme for the
picturesque topographers. Turner endows them with a new
dimension of mystery and grandeur by exaggerating the height
of the hill behind them, and plunging the abbey itself into a rich
and vibrant shade – evidence of his rapidly growing mastery of
the medium of watercolour.

The Pantheon, Oxford Street, the morning after the fire

1792   20 × 25 (516 × 640)

By the age of seventeen, Turner had mastered the architectural
topography that he had been taught by Thomas Malton, and
could send this accomplished example to the Academy
exhibition in 1792. It is a piece of vivid journalism, recording an
event that he had witnessed earlier in the year, and combining
his love of crowds and their varied interests with a perceptive
study of an unusual effect of light: the early sun glows rose-pink
on the icicles created by the firemen's hoses, while firemen and
onlookers fill the street.

A scene in the Welsh mountains with an army on the march

1799 27 × 39⅜ (686 × 1000)

After his second visit to Snowdonia in 1799 Turner seems to have planned a pair of large watercolours on the subject of Edward I's extermination of the Welsh Bards, celebrated in Thomas Gray's famous poem 'The Bard' of 1757. An idyllically Claudean landscape, exhibited in 1800, depicts the Bard surrounded by his followers; the contrasting scene of destruction among the inimical mountains was never finished, but this large sheet was presumably a preparation for it. The vast presences of nature reduce to pigmy insignificance the long straggle of soldiers hunting their helpless prey, who watches (though unseen in this study) on a lofty crag from which, according to Gray's poem, he is shortly to precipitate himself.

The Mer de Glace, Chamonix

1802 12⅜ × 18⅜ (314 × 465)

One of the sketchbooks that Turner took with him to Switzerland in 1802 was the large book that he labelled 'St. Gotthard and Mont Blanc'. He washed its pages with a grey ground before drawing on them, and seems to have chosen subjects that would translate directly into the format of finished compositions; many of the studies were used as the bases for exhibited watercolours or oil paintings. The restricted palette of grey and ochre, amplified with scraping-out for the highlights, is well-suited to the austere landscape of the high Alps, and the book contains some of Turner's most uncompromisingly bleak evocations of mountain scenery, like this stark view of the glacier known as the Sea of Ice above the valley of Chamonix.

A group of Trees beside the Thames

c.1807 $10\frac{1}{8} \times 14\frac{1}{2}$ (257×368)

The watercolour sketches that Turner made along the Thames
after his move to Isleworth in about 1804 count among the most
spontaneous of his studies in the medium, reflecting as they do
the new interest in naturalism that was affecting British artists at
the time. But they betray Turner's innate self-awareness as a
draughtsman, his requirement that every sketch should bear in it
the seeds of a full-blown work. Even this relaxed and unpre-
tentious study is carefully formulated as an abstraction in shades
of black, blue and brownish-green.

Young Anglers

c.1809 $7\frac{1}{2} \times 10\frac{3}{8}$ (183×265)

The *Liber Studiorum* was designed to illustrate Turner's concern
for the whole range of landscape art, from the grandest to the
most informal. In the three issues that appeared during 1811 he
included three plates with subjects showing children's pastimes,
a theme that fascinated him all his life. This one also reflects his
love of fishing, a favourite distraction from the demands of art
and the Academy. It is typical of the brown wash drawings
outlined in pen that he used as the models for the etched and
mezzotinted plates of the series.

The Battle of Fort Rock, Val d'Aosta 1796

1815 $27\frac{3}{8} \times 40$ (696 × 1015)

This complex work was shown at the Academy in 1815 with
Turner's own verses. It is a modern historical subject, and
parallels the 1812 painting of 'Hannibal crossing the Alps' as a
moral statement of the destructive behaviour of man against
man, and the hostility of nature as barrier to man's ambitions.
Napoleon's invasion of Italy is seen as a modern version of
Hannibal's. Like a film director's eye, Turner's sweeps from
foreground group of a countrywoman tending a wounded soldier
to the distant peak of Mont Blanc, eternally indifferent to men's
sufferings.

Perspective Illustration: Pulteney Bridge

c.1810 $26\frac{1}{2} \times 39\frac{5}{8}$ (674 × 1006)

When Turner was appointed Professor of Perspective to the
Royal Academy in 1807 he took his duties very seriously and
read widely in the technical literature to equip himself for the
writing of his lectures. He also made numerous large diagrams
and watercolours to illustrate his remarks. Audiences who found
him a bad lecturer were glad to attend in order to see these
drawings, which often used as examples well-known buildings –
Turner even made a drawing of the interior of the Academy's
exhibition room. This large sheet shows the Palladian Pulteney
Bridge, built in Bath in 1750.

Venice: the Campanile and Doge's Palace

1819 $8\frac{7}{8} \times 11\frac{3}{8}$ (225×289)

One of only four watercolour studies that Turner made on his first visit to Venice in 1819, this is the least concerned with light and atmosphere and concentrates on the formal disposition of the grand buildings that were to figure so prominently in his later paintings of Venice. Indeed, with its bright blue sky and foursquare composition it anticipates the first of those pictures, the homage to Canaletto that Turner was to exhibit in 1833 (see Room 105).

Whitby

1824 $6\frac{1}{2} \times 8\frac{7}{8}$ (158×225)

The Turner Bequest includes two complete series of finished watercolours for the engraver, the *Rivers* and *Ports of England*, published as mezzotint plates in the 1820s. They are characterised by a rich and intense use of watercolour which enables Turner to concentrate the atmospheric range and scale of his larger works within a very small compass. This example, from the *Ports of England*, is a fresh and breezy marine in the tradition of Turner's offshore subjects in oil of the early years of the century.

Shields Lighthouse

*c.*1826 $9\frac{1}{2} \times 11\frac{1}{8}$ (234×283)

Turner's involvement with mezzotint in the long series of plates for the *Liber Studiorum*, and later for the *Rivers* and *Ports of England* led him, in the late 1820s, to experiment with a number of original plates of his own – essays in rich chiaroscuro well suited to the velvety tonal contrasts so typical of the medium. These rare plates were never published; they are known as the 'Little Liber Studiorum'. In preparation for them, Turner made rapid watercolour studies, of which this is one.

A city on a river at sunset

*c.*1832 $5\frac{1}{2} \times 7\frac{3}{8}$ (134×189)

In the 1820s and 30s Turner was occupied with several series of views for engraving; one of the most ambitious was a project to illustrate scenes on the 'Great Rivers of Europe', and he undertook several tours in search of suitable subject-matter. The only work to be published, however, was the three-volume 'French Rivers' set, of 1833–5, covering the Loire and the Seine. The coloured studies and finished drawings for the scheme are on small sheets of blue paper, and exploit a range of vivid and intense colour. This study, brilliantly economical in its evocation of place and atmosphere, was not engraved, and its exact subject is unknown. It has been thought to show either Mainz on the Rhine or Tours on the Loire.

A church spire

*c.*1828 $12\frac{1}{8} \times 19\frac{1}{8}$ (308 × 487)

The Turner Bequest contains numerous colour studies for the great series of *Picturesque Views in England and Wales* on which Turner worked for a decade from 1825. They are often summary generalisations of broad compositional effects – structures of light and colour on to which the elaborate and highly detailed content of the view would later be overlaid. They show that Turner contemplated many subjects that he never realised: this one is perhaps a sketch for a view of Grantham or Newark.

Venice: the Salute from the Calle del Ridotto; night

?1840 $9\frac{7}{8} \times 12$ (250 × 307)

Although Turner took some time to evolve for himself a suitable language in which to express his response to Venice, once he had done so he produced a long outpouring of magical studies celebrating its soft light, its melting atmosphere and vast luminous spaces. The majority are on the white sheets of his roll sketchbooks; but one group of nocturnes uses a darker brown or buff support. A canvas of 1836, 'Juliet and her Nurse', is a view across St. Mark's Square by night, with fireworks, and it is possible that this rapid sketch was executed, from memory, at about the same date; more probably, however, it belongs to Turner's last visit to the city, in 1840.

Edinburgh Castle: the march of the Highlanders

*c.*1836 $3\frac{3}{8} \times 5\frac{1}{2}$ (86 × 140)

In the course of the 1820s and 30s Turner produced illustrations to the works of several contemporary poets: Samuel Rogers, Lord Byron, Thomas Campbell and Walter Scott; as well as to Milton and Bunyan. His designs were intended to be seen in the form of small line-engravings, and are themselves executed on a very small scale. His mastery of watercolour ensured that these conditions offered no obstacles to the expression of ideas as wide-ranging and imaginative as those in any of his larger drawings. The delicate yet intense miniature technique that he had perfected in the *Rivers* and *Ports of England* and other topographical series could be used with equal success to evoke sweeping landscapes within the tiny space of a small octavo page. Many of the illustrations are in vignette form; for the long series of designs he made for the works of Scott in the 1830s he employed both the vignette and full rectangular format. Here, in a drawing only 86 × 140 mm he presents a crowded scene from Scott's *Waverley* that is as atmospheric and full of life as any of his grandest conceptions.

Aldeburgh, Suffolk

*c.*1826 $11 \times 15\frac{3}{4}$ (279 × 400)

The series of *Picturesque Views in England and Wales* on which Turner worked between 1825 and 1835 is in many ways the culmination of his achievement as a watercolourist. It covers a wide range of subject-matter, exploring the relationship between men and their environments in a host of varied settings: towns and villages, sea-coasts and harbours, markets and agricultural valleys, places of resort and places of industry. Moorland, downland, river and mountain form the background to the eternal drama of man's stuggle with nature, his toil and recreation, his terrors and joys. Seas and skies, smoky mornings and golden evenings, storms and calms are all recorded with loving concern for their variety and beauty, in a pictorial language more expressive and powerful than any other evolved in the medium of watercolour. The view of Aldeburgh was one of the earliest to be completed, and was published in 1827.

Zurich : sample study

1841 $9\frac{1}{2} \times 12$ (241 × 304)

Like Venice, the vast spaces of Switzerland inspired Turner to
new outpourings of watercolour studies in the 1840s. Some of
these he elaborated as 'samples' from which he invited patrons to
choose subjects that he could work up as finished watercolours.
This panorama of Zurich, used as the basis for one of the ten
subjects of 1842, exemplifies all Turner's love of the bustling life
of cities. He was to make a second and very similar view of the
same place in a further set of ten executed in 1845. These self-
imposed 'quotas' illustrate the importance for Turner of a
responsive public, and his need to continue working within the
traditional framework of the topographical 'tour'.

Lake Lucerne : sunset : sample study

?1844 $9\frac{1}{2} \times 12$ (244 × 303)

Another of the samples that Turner prepared for his patrons in
the 1840s, affirming once again his love of the Swiss lakes and
mountains, and the infinitely variable light that defines the
spaces around and between them. These late watercolour studies
epitomise the ecstatic contemplations of the ageing artist at
peace with nature and the world.

Wycliffe, near Rokeby

One of the engraved plates from the series of illustrations to
Whitaker's 'History of Richmondshire' on which Turner worked
from 1816 to 1819. The engraver was John Pye, whose print of
Turner's oil painting of 'Pope's Villa' had first opened the
painter's eyes to the expressive possibilities of line engraving.
The rays of light above the Hall were not in Turner's original
drawing, and when asked why he wanted to add them Turner
replied 'That is the place where Wycliffe was born and the light
of the glorious Reformation.' He was always alive to the
historical and human connotations of the places he drew and
sought to reflect them in his treatment of each subject.

The Study Room

The new Study Room in the Clore Gallery is an important addition to the amenities of the Tate. London has already two well-established Print Rooms, at the British Museum and the Victoria and Albert Museum; these both contain, among much else, large collections of works on paper by British artists. The Tate Gallery has acquired drawings and watercolours of the British School only incidentally to its principal task of representing paintings, but over the years has accumulated a fine group ranging from the early eighteenth century to the late nineteenth. Its main strength lies in its holdings of watercolours, which include most of the major practitioners in the medium from Paul Sandby to the Pre-Raphaelites. Nearly all the romantic landscapists of distinction can be found here: Thomas Girtin is represented by the work which is perhaps his masterpiece, 'The White House, Chelsea', and there are examples by De Wint and Cox, the Varleys, Crome and Cotman, Cozens, Stothard, Linnell and Palmer, Bonington and Boys, Callow, Lear and Muller. Of the Victorians Ford Madox Brown, Rossetti, Burne-Jones, Millais, Ruskin and Charles Keene are to be studied in drawings of many different types. The centrepiece of the collection is the outstanding group of works by William Blake, one of the most important in the world, which complements the Turner collection as a comprehensive representation of one of Turner's greatest contemporaries. Constable is also present as a draughtsman, and his collaboration with the mezzotinter David Lucas is recorded in a complete set of the published plates of the *English Landscape Scenery*.

When these works have been displayed in the main galleries of the Tate they have necessarily been seen under restricted lighting. Now that the facilities of a Study Room are available, they can be viewed in the most favourable conditions, with access to works of reference and suitable space for note-taking and research. This does not mean that drawings, watercolours and prints will cease to be displayed in the galleries; but those not on view will be more accessible than they have been in the past. Visitors are welcome to use the Study Room during its opening hours; at other times visits are by appointment. University teachers who wish to bring groups of students for seminar purposes should also make appointments, stating precisely which material they require to use. This will be prepared for them before the arrival of their party, for which an area of the Study Room will be set aside.

Visitors who wish to see material during normal opening hours are requested to deposit all bags in the cloakroom on the ground floor, and to ensure that their hands are clean (a washbasin is provided at the entrance to the Study Room). They should make known to the staff the titles and reference numbers of works they wish to see; these can be ascertained from the catalogue cards and reference books on the open shelves. A form is provided for applications for individual works, and staff will help visitors find the correct registration or catalogue number for purposes of identification. Items requested are brought to the tables, where pencils only are permitted to be used. Sketchbooks by Turner are not normally accessible to students, since they are for the most part extremely fragile. A representative selection of the sketchbooks is on show in the main galleries, and a photographic archive will, it is hoped, supply any information needed, while obviating unnecessary handling. In addition, a microfilm of the Turner Bequest is available.

The purpose of the Study Room is to enable all who are interested in drawings and prints to examine them at leisure in pleasant, quiet surroundings without the inconvenience of controlled lighting or glazing. Drawings are generally mounted in sturdy board mounts which permit handling, though these too should be treated with care. They are stored in solander boxes, which are kept horizontally, and drawings should always be stacked in their boxes when they are not being examined. It is important to avoid touching the surface of a work of art, either with one's hands or with the edge of another mount. When a work is being looked at it should lie flat on the table, or be placed on one of the stands provided; in no case should any work be placed on top of another, except in the solander box. Books of prints are similarly available to visitors on request, and they too should be handled with the greatest care. They should not be placed on stands, but examined flat on the surface of the table.

It is the duty of the Study Room staff to ensure that all items are treated properly, but equally they are there to give assistance, and members of the public are encouraged to ask for guidance. Scholars and art-historians will, of course, avail themselves of the new amenity; but it is hoped that many people other than specialists will take advantage of the opportunity to enjoy the intimate and often very personal works of art that the Study Room contains.